The Holy Rosary of God

To Fr. Rich,
A prolific homilist
we are blessed to have
here at St. Daniel's!

— Gus

The Holy Rosary of God

PALMETTO
PUBLISHING

Charleston, SC
www.PalmettoPublishing.com

The Holy Rosary of God

Copyright © 2021 by Gustavo Vertiz

All rights reserved.

No portion of this book may be reproduced, stored in a retrieval system, or transmitted in any form by any means–electronic, mechanical, photocopy, recording, or other–except for brief quotations in printed reviews, without prior permission of the author.

First Edition

Paperback ISBN: 978-1-63837-398-8
eBook ISBN: 978-1-63837-428-2

Obsequium Religiosum
The author of this book believes and assents with absolute submission of mind and will to the authentic Magisterium of the Roman Catholic Church, and reverently recognizes the judgments of the Roman Pontiff, accepting them sincerely *in toto*. The author humbly requests a quick fraternal correction of any unintentional error conflicting with Catholic doctrine is found in this book.

*I'd like to thank my wife and family for their support
and helping me to become a better father*

Table of Contents

Introduction · ix

Chapter 1   A Brief History of the Holy Rosary · · · · · · · · · · · · · 1

Chapter 2   Popes who loved the Holy Rosary · · · · · · · · · · · · · · 6

Chapter 3   Saints devoted to the Holy Rosary · · · · · · · · · · · · · · 9

Chapter 4   Apparitions of the Blessed Mother · · · · · · · · · · · · · 12

Chapter 5   A Prodigal Son · 17

Chapter 6   Steps on how to pray the Rosary · · · · · · · · · · · · · · · 23

Chapter 7   Various ways to pray the Holy Rosary · · · · · · · · · · · 35

Chapter 8   Promises from Heaven · 41

Chapter 9   Mystical Rose · 47

Epilogue   · 55

References   · 57

Introduction

The Holy Rosary is a beautiful jewel from heaven! When you pray the Holy Rosary you are spiritually holding the Blessed Mother's hand. In this little book, we will cover a brief overview of the origin of the Holy Rosary, but more important it will inform you and hopefully encourage you to consider what's being presented and take action yourself.

Things the book will cover include: Why should we pray the Rosary? There are countless reasons. How should we pray the Rosary? There are many ways. What do the popes and saints have to say about the Holy Rosary? What are the promises it makes? There are many treasures to be found in it. Our Blessed Mother tells us which ones she will keep with us while we live, when we evangelize, and when we die. In addition, she wants to bring us closer to a deeper love of her Son, Our Lord Jesus Christ, and of course do His Will. Remember, Our Lady said, "Do whatever He tells you." (John 2:5).

However, it would be remiss if we didn't include a brief summary of Our Lady as referenced by a Doctor of the Church, St. Alphonsus Liguori, in *The Glories of Mary* and also in a four volume book by Venerable Mary of Ágreda in *The Mystical City of God*. That title reminds me of one of my favorite titles, "Mystical Rose" in the Litany of Loreto. This brief summary is to give prominence to consider asking Our Blessed Mother to be the queen of our lives. Our Lady always brings us to her

Son, Our Lord Jesus Christ, and she brings Him through the Eucharist. For example, as you will learn more about the Blessed Mother it will become apparent that in apparitions she sometimes asks for churches to be built in her name. Although the parish or chapel might be named after her, its central purpose is to offer Jesus Himself in the Eucharist in all the masses offered at that parish. Mission accomplished!

There is so much to know about our Catholic faith, and the many ways one can learn more—through books (especially the Bible), videos, and even websites, for we know in today's world we can access all this information in a digital format. I certainly do—everything from reading books on an e-reader to watching videos on faith topics using YouTube, and even for church services or the Rosary, as well as to look up general information online on our Catholic faith. I've heard our faith described as approaching a banquet buffet with many things to choose from, it's so rich and varied! As they say, knowing Our God is fathomless. Our priests and religious leaders are there to guide us, however in this book we will focus on the Holy Rosary, for it is so important for our faith. Of first importance is the Holy Mass, second are the Sacraments, and third is the Holy Rosary. We'll review how to use some or all of the media mentioned to help you pray the Rosary wherever you are, physically and mentally. I say mentally, because as I write, we are living in the time of Covid and some of us might be anxious, stressed, or depressed, etc. All the more reason to pray the Rosary.

CHAPTER 1
A Brief History of the Holy Rosary

For whoever finds me, finds life and obtains the favor of the Lord.
(Proverb 8:35)

The Holy Rosary is a beautiful gift from the Holy Trinity given to Our Blessed Mother. Originally, according to the book *Secrets of the Holy Rosary* by St. Louis de Montfort, "The Rosary is composed, principally and in substance, of the prayer Christ and the Angelic Salutation, that is the Our Father and the Hail Mary. It was without a doubt the first prayer and the principal devotion of the faithful and has been in use all through the centuries from the time of the apostles and disciples down to the present. It had always been called the Psalter of Jesus and Mary. The difference is the Psalter (Psalms) is the sign of the One who is to come, the Rosary proclaims Him as having come. That is how they began to call their prayer of 150 Salutations (15 decades=150 Hail Marys) the Psalter (Rosary) of Mary, to precede each decade with an Our Father."[1]

That is the beginning of the Rosary as given by God. Our Lady, according to tradition, then gave the Rosary to St. Dominic in the 12th century, who was eventually credited as the founder of the Holy Rosary and also became the founder of the Dominicans. At the time of her appearance to him, St. Dominic was feeling demoralized in trying to convert the Albigensians, who were spreading errors about the Catholic faith. St. Dominic was blessed by this gift of the Holy Rosary from the Blessed Mother, to teach the Mysteries (the Life of Christ) from it and eventually to convert the Albigensians. She taught him to use the Rosary as a spiritual weapon. Our Lady will teach us, too, when we pray it.

The prayers that compose the Rosary are arranged in sets of ten Hail Marys, called decades. In St. Louis De Montfort's book *The Secrets of the Holy Rosary*, he says, "Our Lady's Rosary is divided into three crowns of five decades each for the following reasons:

- To honor the three persons of the Holy Trinity
- Honor the life, death, and glory of Jesus Christ
- To imitate the Triumphant Church (Heaven) to help the members of the militant Church (the living) and alleviate the Church suffering (Purgatory)
- To imitate the three groups into which the prayers are divided: the first for the purgative life (purify from sin), the second for the illuminative life (practicing virtue) and the third for the unitive life (union with God through love).
- To give us abundant graces during life, peace in death and glory in eternity."[2] How beautiful is this gift from heaven for us mortals! First, to give honor and glory to the Holy Trinity, second, to give honor and glory to our Blessed Mother, Queen of Heaven, and third, to sanctify ourselves—that is, to set ourselves apart for God's special use and purpose.

A Brief History of the Holy Rosary

The Rosary means "a crown of roses," as Blessed Alan de la Roche said, and every time we devoutly pray a Hail Mary we create a beautiful rose for Our Lady. When we complete a Rosary we make a crown of roses, and are spiritually placing those crowns on the heads of Jesus and Mary.[3] As mentioned above, there are so many graces one can get by praying the Rosary. To give honor, and to pray for sinners everywhere, for ourselves, loved ones, extended family, friends, coworkers, enemies, aborted babies, poor souls, our priests, the religious, the Holy Father, and nowadays protection from the Covid virus. The list is endless. How can we walk away from praying the Rosary for all these needful things? Many beautiful things happen when we pray the Rosary. Let us dedicate our whole lives to praying the Rosary every day.

Yes, Our Lady's gift is the sword, our spiritual weapon to wage war against the Devil. The demons flee when the names of Our Lord and the Mother of God are pronounced when praying the Rosary. Today with so much evil in the world, more prayer warriors are needed to combat the spiritual warfare waged on the soul of every living person.

It is a matter of life (living with God) and death (being with God forever), every day in the spiritual world. Unknowingly, a war is being waged for your soul, your loved ones, and humanity in general. Not only should we pick up our cross daily and follow Jesus, but we should take action by praying the Rosary, to protect ourselves and our loved ones from the Evil One and his minions. You might think, as some others, that praying the Rosary is for the elderly, mostly women. Although that is partially true, for some do love to pray the Rosary as we get closer to our demise, but adult men, women (including religious orders), and the young, all pray the Rosary.

Some people object to the repetition of the Hail Mary prayers as monotonous. The Venerable Bishop Fulton J. Sheen, in his book *The World's First Love, Mary, Mother of God*, articulated it best.

"When we say the Rosary, we say to God, the Holy Trinity, to the Incarnate Savior, to the Blessed Mother, I love you, I love you, I love you!"[4]

During the great wars there were many soldiers who knelt with their chaplains to pray the Rosary before going to the battlefield and possibly meeting their deaths. They were real men. Fathers or heads of households also have a great responsibility to protect their families spiritually. It has been said that the devil wants to get the heads of families out of the way, for once that happens he can attack the young. Will you be a prayer warrior?

A veteran would recall during WWII, of being in combat all night long and saying rosaries to give them courage. An airman tells this story that during WWII in 1940 there was a squadron leader who was admired by his squadron as a great leader setting the example even in praying the rosary as he bunked with them. The squadron learned the rosary and eventually joined him even though some were not Catholic. He gave them all rosaries as they were leaving for night raids from England over Germany. He said, "We shall be in some tight situations, but then if you agree, we'll say the Rosary. If you will promise to keep the Rosary with you always throughout your life and to say it, I can promise you that Our Lady will bring you all back safe to Canada." They answered, "Sure thing."

※

"Little did we dream we would be in action for four years, many times in dreadful danger with fire all around us. ...How many hundreds of Rosaries we must have said. After two years it was noted that ours was the only squadron that had not lost a plane nor a single life. We said nothing, but we knew." The kicker as he finishes his story: "So I never forget to keep my Rosary with me and say it everyday although I am not Catholic." You can catch this great story here:

traditionalcatholicpriest.com/2014/10/07/
marys-holy-rosary-in-the-second-world-war/

Why is the Rosary placed with such importance after Holy Mass and the Sacraments? That will be explained later in the book. However, if you go online to <u>Through Mary</u> (www.ThroughMary.com) you will find the headings for Our Lady: "Mary is our Spiritual Mother," "Mary is the Spouse of the Holy Spirit," "Mary can make crosses into something sweet," "Mary is the Quickest way to holiness," "Mary sanctifies our good actions," "Mary helps us to be humble," and finally, "Mary brings us to the Fountain of Mercy." It says that praying the Holy Rosary is our way of spiritually communicating with our Mother to ask her for graces and blessings, for it crosses into something sweet and sanctifies our actions.

Our Lady as "Mediatrix" can take our muddled, sometimes incoherent, prayers and turn them into a beautiful bouquet that's presented to the Holy Trinity. In addition, the website calls us to consecrate ourselves as soon as possible to her Immaculate Heart, which, you will find, is an act that will come naturally as you pray your Rosary daily, and then you will be all hers. How wonderful!

CHAPTER 2

Popes who loved the Holy Rosary

⚜

*Blessed art thou, O Daughter, by the Lord
most high God, above all women on earth*
(Judith 13:23)

There were popes throughout the history of the Catholic faith who were totally devoted to praying the Rosary daily. They prayed the Rosary to help them overcome the trials and tribulations they encountered in their times, to evangelize and proclaim the Kingdom of God to the multitude, and to educate the faithful on the graces of praying Rosary and the quickest way to sanctity. At the University of Dayton website All About Mary (www.udayton.edu/imri/all-about-mary.php) you will find the article "Popes on the Rosary" under the main heading "All about Mary." There, you will find the following papal quotes and observations.

POPE PIUS THE XII (1939-1958)

'We do not hesitate to affirm publicly we put great confidence in the Holy Rosary for the healing of evils of our times."

POPE PIUS X (1903–1914)

The Rosary is the most beautiful and the richest of all prayers to the Mediatrix of all grace. It is the prayer that touches most the heart of the Mother of God. Pray it each day."

POPE LEO XII (1878–1903)

also viewed the Rosary as a vital means to participate in the life of Mary and to find the way to Christ.

POPE JOHN XXIII (1958–1963)

'The Rosary is the glory of the Roman Church. It takes its place... after the Mass and the Sacraments."

POPE BENEDICT XVI (2005–2013)

'In praying the Rosary, we follow **His Holiness Benedict XVI**, *who prays it with frequency each morning and uses it to contemplate with Mary the face of Christ."*

POPE JOHN PAUL II (1978–2005)

'The Rosary is my favorite prayer. Pray, pray much, Say the Rosary everyday. Recite the Rosary every day. I earnestly urge Pastors to pray the Rosary and to teach people in their Christian communities how to pray it." Also to note, in 2002 the great **John Paul II** *added the Luminous Mysteries to the Rosary. In his Apostolic Letter, the Holy Pontiff called them 'the Mysteries of Light."*

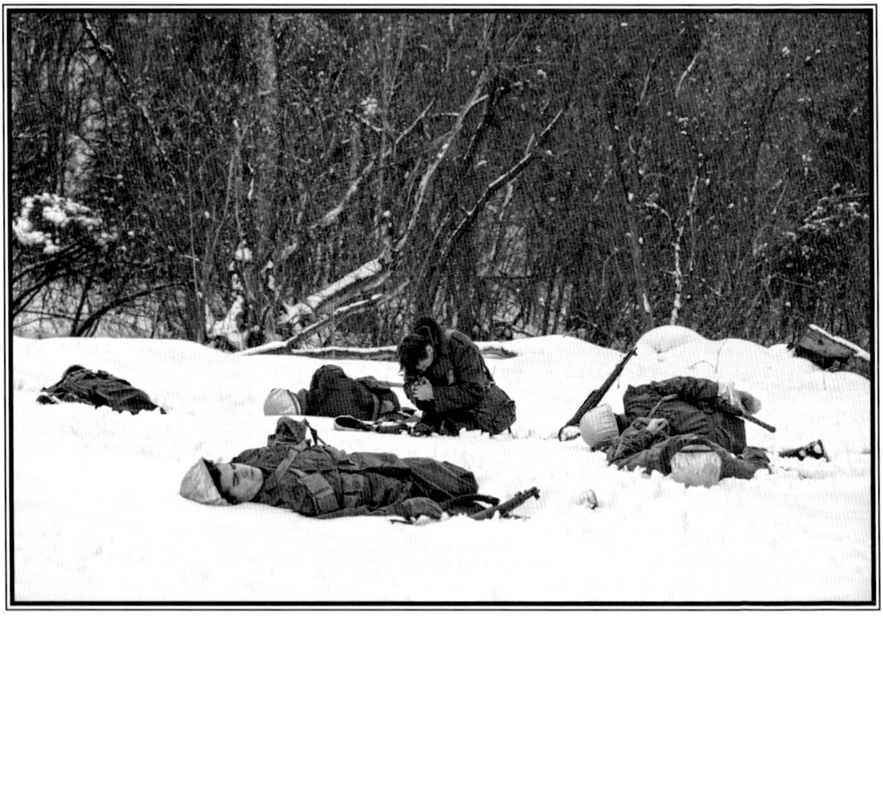

CHAPTER 3
Saints devoted to the Holy Rosary

❦

For He so magnified thy name this day, that thy praise shall not depart out of the mouths of men.
(Judith 13:25)

In every nation which shall hear thy name the God of Israel shall be magnified on occasion of thee.
(Judith 13:31)

If you go online and type in "Saints who prayed the Rosary" you will find a website called Aleteia (www.aleteia.org). There they have a list of saints who are noted for having a deep devotion to the Blessed Mother and the Rosary. Here are a few to illustrate the point that, if our goal is Heaven, in order to attain sanctity in this life we need to remember what Pope John XIII said: "Devote yourself to attendance at Mass (daily if possible), the sacraments (especially ongoing monthly Confession), and praying the Rosary devoutly will help tremendously as signs of your destiny toward Heaven."

The Aleteia website states: "These holy men and women believed there was great power in reciting the traditional Catholic prayer. While the Rosary is largely viewed as a boring and monotonous form of prayer, countless men and women would beg to differ, and have found in it a plethora of Graces from God. In particular, the Rosary has provided rich spiritual nourishment to many saints over the years, testifying to the instrumental role the Rosary can have in a person's life."

SAINTS DEVOTED TO THE ROSARY

St. Louis-Marie de Montfort (1673-1716) was a preacher and was created a missionary apostolic by Pope Clement XI. His feast day is April 28th. St. Louis is well known for his deep devotion to the Blessed Mother, and famous for his prayer "*Totus Tuus ego sum*" which means "I am all yours." One of his books, *True Devotion to the Blessed Virgin*, is considered a classic. His other book, *Secrets of the Rosary*, is highly esteemed for his devotion to the Holy Rosary of Our Lady. He says, "Never will anyone who says his Rosary every day be led astray. This is a statement that I would gladly sign with my blood. The Son of God became man for our salvation, but only in Mary and through Mary."

St. Padre Pio of Pietrelcina (1887-1968) was well known for having the stigmata—wounds of Christ—and was considered a mystic because of his gift of reading souls. Imagine him being your pastor! He was also known for his ability to bilocate, and for his healing powers. These gifts of God to Padre Pio were as much a torment of suffering to him as they were a blessing. He wrote, "Her Rosary is the weapon against the evils of the world today. All Graces given by God pass through the Blessed Mother. Some people are so foolish that they think they can go through life without the help of the Blessed Mother. Love the Madonna and pray the Rosary, for her Rosary is the weapon against the evils of the world today. All Graces given by God pass through the Blessed Mother."

In his early years before his ministry, **St. Francis de Sales (1567-1622)** prayed the *"Memorare"* before a statue of the Black Madonna. He then consecrated himself to the Blessed Mother and dedicated his life to God. St. Francis was considered a spellbinding preacher. He preached with such fervor and dedication that in the town of Chablais, France, where the majority were Calvinists, he converted almost the entire population of 72,000 in four years, and they came back to the Catholic Faith. He said, "The greatest method of praying is to pray the Rosary."

We can't forget **St. Dominic (1170-1221)**, the founder of the Rosary. Clearly, St. Dominic was a giant in the Catholic Faith. He attained his sanctity through his obedience to Our Lord and Blessed Mother, and his devotion to the practice of praying the Rosary, which became a blessing to him for founding the Dominican Order. "One day, through the Rosary and the Scapular, Our Lady will save the world." Those words St. Dominic said were prophetic, as Our Lady said at Fatima in 1917, "But in the end my Immaculate Heart will triumph."

St. Alphonsus Liguori (1696-1787) was a bishop, a Doctor of the Church, founder of the Redemptorists Order, and had countless other accomplishments. Well known as a confessor, his confessional was always crowded, with many habitual sinners returning to the Church and its sacraments. St. Alphonsus wrote *The Glories of Mary*. He writes, "It is more efficacious to say the Rosary in company with others, than to say it alone."[5]

CHAPTER 4
Apparitions of the Blessed Mother

I shall put enmity between you and the woman, and between your offspring and hers; it will bruise your head and you will strike its heel.
(Genesis 3:15)

I am the Mother of fair love, and of fear, and of knowledge and Holy Hope
(Sirach 24:24)

REASONS TO PRAY THE HOLY ROSARY

At this point, you still might not be motivated to pray the Rosary. Although I thank you for reading this far, let's review some reasons why you would want to pray the Rosary based on the apparitions of our Blessed Mother and what she said or did regarding the Rosary.

There are hundreds of reported apparitions dating back to the first apparition, which was Our Lady of the Pillar in Zaragoza, Spain, in 40 AD. This apparition took place during the earthly life of the Mother of God. Standing on a pillar, she appeared with the Child Jesus to the Apostle St. James the Elder while he was living and preaching in Spain. She came to his aid with his evangelization of the people of Hispania.

Apparitions have also taken place in the 20th and 21st century. This book will focus on just apparitions of the Blessed Mother that pertain to the Rosary. Please note, apparitions are considered private revelation, which means you decide whether you believe it or not. Public revelation, however, we must believe because it belongs to the Deposit of Faith of the Catholic Church. The Catechism of the Catholic Church, CCC 67, defines both private and public revelation. Although some apparitions are private, there have been bishops and popes who have strongly approved and encouraged the faithful to follow and believe the messages in these apparitions. Going to the Wikipedia page for Marian Apparitions (www.wikipedia.org/wiki/List_of_Marian_apparitions), as well as on other websites, you will find a list of these apparitions of Our Lady.

APPARITIONS OF OUR LADY

Our Lady of Guadalupe in 1531, Feast Day December 12
This apparition of Our Lady is included because, although she did not speak of the Rosary, the fact is Our Lady left with Juan Diego for proof a rare image of herself on a tilma, a cloak made of cactus fiber, a rarity to happen, as the last time was back in 40 AD.

Our Lady requested a Church to be built and eventually caused the massive conversion of people in Mexico to the Catholic faith. In addition, it led to a deep devotion of this image of her in the Americas, as well as being invoked by thousands of devotees throughout the world. Our Lady of Guadalupe is patron of the unborn, so at times a copy of her image has been carried to be prayed with at abortion clinics.

Our Lady of Fatima in 1917, Memorial May 13

Probably the most famous apparition of Our Lady where she speaks of the Rosary is in this apparition. She is called "Our Lady of the Rosary." During the apparition, Our Lady asks three children, Jacinta, Francisco, and Lucia, to pray the Rosary for peace in the world, to end the war (World War II), and for the conversion of sinners, who at that time deeply offended Our Lord and the Immaculate Heart of Mary. As you might imagine, the sins of today are deeply offending Our Lord and Our Blessed Mother. Reparation is needed, and praying the Rosary is what Our Lady requests to combat the evil and convert sinners. Such is the power of the Rosary. The most dramatic part of this apparition was the vision of Hell which Our Lady permitted the children to experience, and which is, in essence, meant for us today to be reminded of the reality of Hell. Saints and theologians have also described the reality of Purgatory and its many levels of suffering.

In our Catholic faith, Purgatory is a temporary place. The soul is purified there and waits to be taken up to heaven by Our Lord. Rosary prayers can help those poor souls. However, do we actually know what it means to spend time in Purgatory? "But do not forget this one thing, dear friends: With the Lord a day is like a thousand years, and a thousand years are like a day." (2 Peter 3:8).

If you'd like to learn about the suffering you may incur if you go to Purgatory, go online and take a look at this YouTube video about the Levels of Purgatory (www.youtube.com/watch?v=Pu1I9J_vEYQ). One of the fifteen promises for praying the Rosary daily is—as described later in the book—Our Lady will deliver you from Purgatory.

Our Lady of Lourdes in 1858, Feast day February 11

This is a well known apparition, as the film *The Song of Bernadette* made Our Lady's apparition well loved. Although Our Lady did not speak of the Rosary implicitly, what is of importance is her title as the "Immaculate

Conception" and that she was dressed in white, bearing a "golden Rosary" and a blue belt around her waist. Our Blessed Mother always calls us to conversion, to pray the Rosary, to fast, and to do penance.

Our Lady of the Rosary of San Nicolas in 1983
This is a more recent apparition in Buenos Aires, Argentina, approved by the Argentinian Bishop as being supernatural in origin. Our Lady appeared to a housewife named Gladys as she was praying her Rosary at home. Our Lady handed Gladys a white Rosary. The messages given were of things to come if the world does not convert...and I'd like to add, and repent.

Our Lady of Medjugorje in 1981 and ongoing
The apparition has not been approved by the Holy See. Our Lady appeared to six teenagers, who are now adults and some are married. This apparition has yielded much fruit, from small miracles of rosaries turning to gold, miracles of the sun, to the conversion of great sinners. I give witness to my own 2nd conversion, as my first was baptism, and my second brought me back to the Catholic faith toward the end of the 1980s.

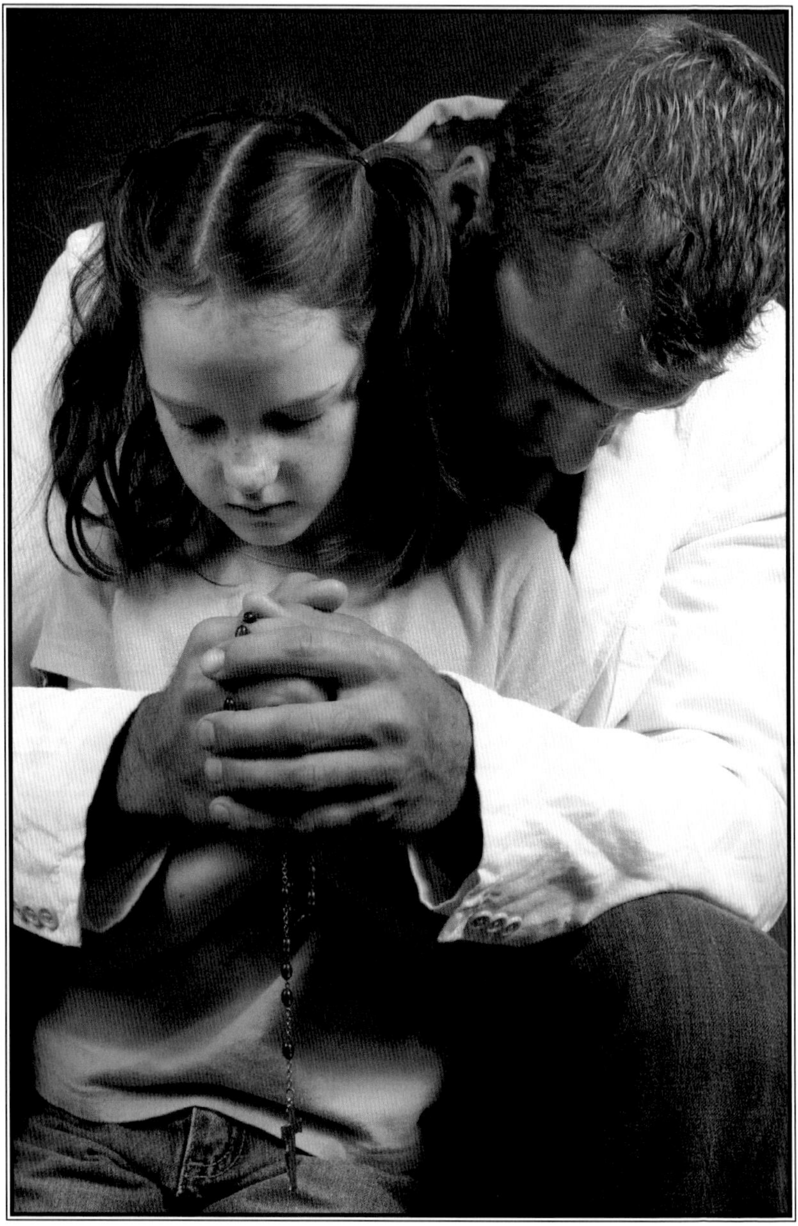

CHAPTER 5
A Prodigal Son

*And a great sign appeared in heaven,
a woman clothed with the sun.*
(Revelations 12:1)

*Hear, O' Daughter, by the Lord most high
God, above all women on earth*
(Judith 13:23)

There were six in my family when I was growing up. My parents gave me a strong foundation for my Catholic faith. I remember while going to St. Ann Catholic grammar school in Dallas, Texas, we always had a yearly children's procession in the schoolyard in May to crown our Blessed Mother as Queen of Heaven. We sang Marian songs such as "On this day, O Beautiful Mother." It was an innocent time. Our family moved to Chicago when I was eleven, an opportune time for the Devil to slowly pull me away from my faith with his lies as I grew up roaming the streets. My teenage years, despite Catholic high school at St. Rita's, did not keep me on the narrow road with God. Wandering in a spiritual desert later in my college years, I lost myself in the illusions of the times during the 1960s, 1970s, and the 1980s when it finally ended. Unfortunately, getting back my faith took the death of my mother. I recall seeing my mother as she was dying of cancer, and she was protecting herself by continually making the sign of the cross as she lay on her bed, her eyes closed, during her last hours at home. She knew she would soon pass away and was getting ready to cross over. Thankfully, she did receive the Last Rites. But that memory of my mom was sealed in my brain. As I said when speaking at my mom's funeral, she showed us how to live in the faith and how to die in the faith.

Not long after my mom passed away, one day at home with my wife and my little girls I was watching a short documentary on TV about Medjugorje, a village in Bosnia and Herzegovina, showing young seers kneeling and looking up in prayer as the apparition of Our Lady was actually happening. A female voiceover was used for Our Lady, telling of her message at that moment. The voice was soft and sweet, and it seemed to me as if the Blessed Mother was actually talking to me personally. It's difficult to explain what really happened. All I know is, in those moments I was recalling all my past failures before my God and I wept. All through a TV documentary!

There could have been countless others who had the same experience. That is the power of God, and the brilliance of our Blessed Mother to reach multitudes by appearing at Medjugorje. She's always leading us back to her Son.

I fell away from God for many years, but now it was our Blessed Mother who was bringing me back to my faith. It was a redemption that caused me to pray the Rosary daily, which I had hardly done before. I took bible study and, of course, I went to Holy Mass and Confession as I became a practicing Catholic. My wife and I were then blessed with two more children.

At times there are those of us who, as we age, go through mini apocalypses as we cycle up and down with our faith. Sometimes we go forward, or we slide back and then forward again. Gratefully, Our Lord loves a penitent heart, because it is through our weakness that He shows His strength. Through Our Lord's Mercy we are called to have a burning fire of love. It's worth noting that monthly Confession can work wonders for us to stay on a straight and narrow path.

And now these three remain: faith, hope, and love. But the greatest of these is love. (1Cor 13:13).

God's wisdom invites us into this interwoven circle of love of the Holy Trinity. And it is our Blessed Mother who partakes in the midst of God's love as the Daughter of God the Father, Mother of Our Lord Jesus Christ, and Spouse of the Holy Spirit. It stands to reason that St. Louis de Montfort wrote in short, "Jesus through Mary."

It is precisely those Graces of God's Love through the Blessed Mother that bring me back to a deeper love of the Lord as I pray the Rosary, and also ask her with faith, hope, and love to be worthy of her promises and of Our Lord's. These promises will be outlined a bit later in this little book.

※

This next prayer said daily is a Godsend. It was given to us by St. Alphonsus Liguori, and it can give us fortitude to endure to the end of life, because we may backslide to our old ways and never come back, as happened to Judas. We want to end as St. Paul expressed it: "I have fought the good fight, I have finished the race, I have kept the faith." (2 Timothy 4:6-22).

Here is the St. Alphonsus prayer:

The Holy Rosary of God

Prayer to obtain Final Perseverance

Eternal Father, I humbly adore Thee, and thank Thee for having redeemed me through Jesus Christ. I thank Thee most sincerely for having made me a Christian, by giving me the true faith, and by adopting me as Thy son, in the sacrament of baptism. I thank Thee for having, after the numberless sins I had committed, waited for my repentance, and for having pardoned all the offences which I have offered to Thee, and for which I am now sincerely sorry, because they have been displeasing to Thee, who art Infinite Goodness. I thank Thee for having preserved me from so many relapses of which I would have been guilty if Thou hadst not protected me. But my enemies still continue, and will continue till death, to combat against me, and to endeavor to make me their slave. If Thou dost not constantly guard and succor me with Thy aid, I, a miserable creature, shall return to sin, and shall certainly lose Thy grace. I beseech Thee, then, for the love of Jesus Christ, to grant me holy perseverance unto death. Jesus, Thy Son, has promised that Thou wilt grant whatsoever we ask in his name. Through the merits, then, of Jesus Christ, I beg, for myself and for all the just, the grace never again to be separated from Thy love, but to love Thee forever, in time and eternity. Mary, Mother of God, pray to Jesus for me. Amen.

You can find the St. Alphonsus prayer, and many others, at <u>Sensus Fidelium</u> (www.sensusfidelium.us/meditations)

My oldest daughter has two children, her son who is in Pre-K attends a Catholic grammar school. The teacher encourages the class to pray the rosary with their family. It would be wonderful to hear more Catholic grammar schools doing the same.

One of my sisters shared with me, before I was born in Dallas, my mom in her strife moved in with her five children to live with her oldest sister who had a big house. My aunt at that time was very devoted to the Blessed Mother and had a wall statue of Her. At about 6 pm every evening was Rosary time. The front door was kept open and if any child looked in or tried to walk by, my great aunt would just nod to them and they knew they had to come in and kneel and join the Rosary. I wonder how many Catholic grandparents, or elder extended family, teaching the young to pray the Rosary?

My sister who always prayed the Rosary, would faithfully pray it to give her strength and faith as my brother-in-law was recently hospitalized several times and doctors could not diagnose his illnesses accurately. It was a stressful time and much prayer was needed. I also learned from her that in Dallas before covid, at Our Lady of Guadalupe Cathedral, the Rosary was prayed before the Spanish Sunday Mass. It's unfortunate more parishes don't pray the Rosary on Sunday.

My other sister, when I asked her why she prayed the Rosary, said it was because her mother told her to pray it. That is the Blessed Mother told her. This was four years ago when she first consecrated herself to the Blessed Mother using the St Louis De Monfort Consecration. Her parish priest asked her Rosary church group to learn the Rosary in Latin. They did and now pray the Rosary in Latin and she says she loves it! Is Latin Rosary on its way back?

Over a year ago my sister had to quickly get her husband to the emergency room and he was then hospitalized and had surgery. He was then comatose in bed for weeks because of heavy medications. She practically lived in his hospital room with a small overnight bag for a time.

The Holy Rosary of God

Sleeping in a chair, she would rise at 5am, get something to eat, then head to chapel and pray her Rosary for support. She would then sit with her husband as he lay there and would hold his hand and hold the rosary in the other hand to pray. There was now support for the both of them.

CHAPTER 6

Steps on how to pray the Rosary

So now, children, listen to me; instruction and wisdom do not reject!
(Proverbs 8:32–33)

And the moon was under feet, and upon her head a crown of twelve stars.
(Rev. 12:1).

If you are not familiar with the basics of praying the Rosary, I will outline them now. The Rosary's core prayers are the Our Father and ten Hail Marys.

If you do know how to pray the Rosary and already know the Mysteries, do not pass Go and do not collect $200. Sorry, I digress! If that's the case, I suggest scrolling down to the chapter titled "Various Ways to Pray The Rosary."

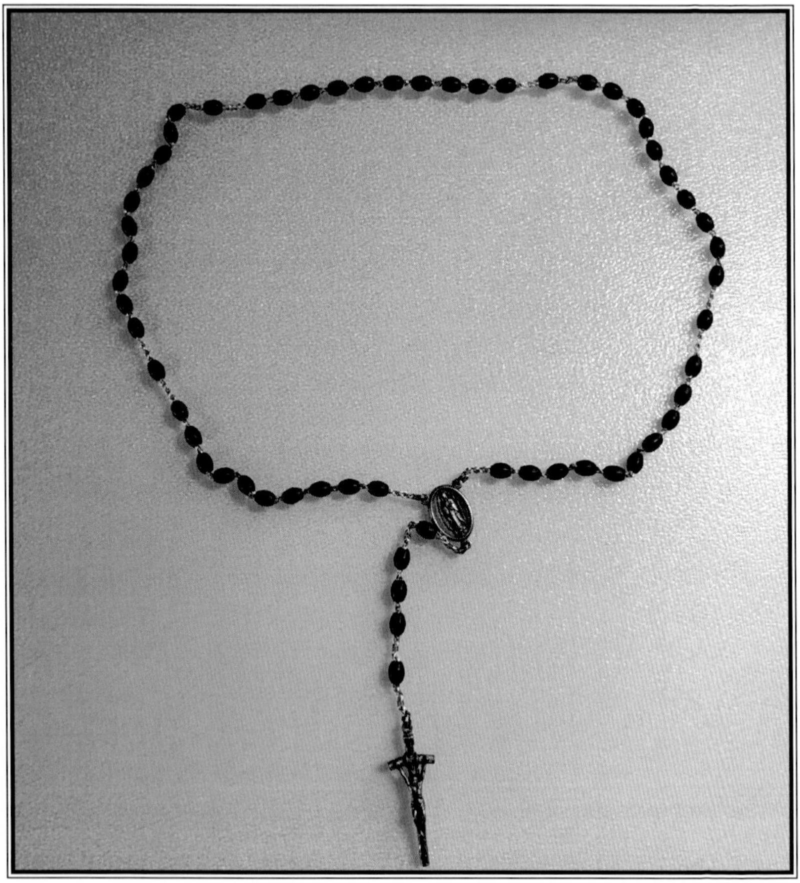

THE BASIC STEPS

I will review the prayers in the next section. Here is the order they are said:

The Rosary is begun on the short strand. Start by selecting the first bead after the crucifix and reciting the Apostles Creed. Second, at the first large bead, you pray one Our Father. Next are three Hail Marys, said for the virtues: Hail Mary Faith, Hail Mary Hope, Hail Mary Charity. Your Rosary may have an extra bead before the decades, or not. Either way, this is when you pray the Fatima prayer.

The praying of the decades follows, repeating the cycle for each mystery. Start by announcing the First Mystery, then pray one Our Father on the large bead, ten Hail Marys, Glory Be in the space before the next large bead, along with the Fatima prayer. At the next decade announce the second Mystery, and repeat the steps above. Continue the Rosary until you complete all five decades reciting the five Mysteries. You then conclude with the Hail Holy Queen and any other intentions, then the sign of the Cross. That's the basics.

THE PRAYERS

Always begin sincerely by making the sign of the Cross as you are entering into the company of the Celestial Choir: In the name of the Father and of the Son and of the Holy Spirit. Amen.

Pray the Apostles Creed

I believe in God, the Father Almighty, Creator of Heaven and earth, and in Jesus Christ, His only Son, Our Lord, Who was conceived by the Holy Spirit, born of the Virgin

Mary, suffered under Pontius Pilate, was crucified, died and was buried. He descended into Hell; and on the third day He rose again from the dead. He ascended into Heaven and sitteth at the right hand of God , the Father Almighty, from thence He shall come to judge the living and the dead. I believe in the Holy Spirit, the holy Catholic Church, the communion of saints, the forgiveness of sins, the resurrection of the body and life everlasting. Amen.

Pray Our Father

Our Father, Who art in Heaven, Hallowed be Thy Name. Thy Kingdom come. Thy Will be done, on earth as it is in Heaven. Give us this day our daily bread. And forgive us our trespasses, as we forgive those who trespass against us. And lead us not into temptation, but deliver us from evil. Amen.

Pray Hail Mary,
one on each of three beads:

Hail Mary full of grace, the Lord is with thee, Blessed art thou among women and blessed is the fruit of thy womb, Jesus. Holy Mary, Mother of God, pray for us sinners, now and at the hour of our death. Amen.

Pray Glory Be

Glory Be to the Father, and to the Son, and to the Holy Spirit. As it was in the beginning, is now, and ever shall be, world without end. Amen.

Pray the Fatima Prayer

O' My Jesus, forgive us our sins, save us from the fires of Hell, lead all souls to Heaven, especially those most in need of Thy Mercy. Also pray this for the poor souls in Purgatory.

You will recall that Hail Marys are arranged in sets of ten, called decades. You now pray the five decades, repeating the same cycle for each Mystery, listed below. Start with the first decade, beginning with one Our Father, followed by ten Hail Marys, and one Glory Be, and you may end with the Fatima Prayer.

Following is a review of the Mysteries. In a group setting and if you are the leader, they are each announced before each decade. Or, another group participant can lead the decade for the group.

The Mysteries of the Holy Rosary

Traditionally, the Rosary divides the life of Jesus into three sections called Mysteries, the essential Mysteries of Scripture. In 2002, Pope John Paul II recommended an additional set. They are:

The Holy Rosary of God

The Joyful Mysteries, said on Mondays and Saturdays
The Sorrowful Mysteries, said on Tuesdays and Fridays
The Glorious Mysteries, said on Wednesdays and Sundays
The Luminous Mysteries, said on Thursdays

You need only announce the title, the description is optional.

The Joyful Mysteries

The Annunciation – Angel Gabriel announces
Mary to be the Mother of God.
The Visitation – Mary visits her cousin Elizabeth
The Nativity – Our Lord is born on Christmas
The Presentation – Our Lord as an infant
is presented at the Temple
The Finding in the Temple – Our Lord as a child
was lost and now found in the Temple

The Sorrowful Mysteries

The Agony in the Garden – The start of Our Lord's
Passion starting in the Garden of Gethsemane
The Scourging at the Pillar – Jesus is stripped and severely scourged
The Crowning with Thorns – Jesus is mocked of His Kingship
The Carrying of the Cross – Jesus carries His Cross to Calvary
The Crucifixion – Jesus is nailed to the Cross at Calvary and dies.

Steps on how to pray the Rosary

The Glorious Mysteries

The Resurrection – Jesus Christ is risen
The Ascension – Jesus ascends to Heaven
The Descent of the Holy Spirit – The Holy Spirit descends upon the Apostles
The Assumption – Our Blessed Mother taken up to Heaven, body and soul
The Coronation – Our Blessed Mother is crowned as Queen of Heaven

The Luminous Mysteries

The Baptism of Our Lord – Jesus is baptized by John the Evangelist
The Wedding at Cana – Jesus performs His first Miracle
The Proclamation of the Kingdom – The sermon on the Mount by Jesus
The Transfiguration – Jesus's Divinity proclaimed on Mount Tabor
The Institution of the Eucharist – Jesus in the Eucharist

Praying the Litany of Loreto at the end of a Rosary has long been a Catholic prayer tradition. When we pray it in church after the Rosary, we ask again for her intercession and to give honor to Our Lady, especially in times when we hear of the desecration of her image or statue, or that of Our Lord.

Litany of Loreto (Blessed Virgin Mary)

Lord, have mercy on us,
Christ, have mercy on us,
Lord, have mercy on us, Christ hear us.
Christ, graciously hear us.
God, the Father of heaven.
Have mercy on us.
God, the Son, Redeemer of the world:
Have mercy on us.
God, the Holy Ghost,
Have mercy on us.
Holy Trinity, One God,
Have mercy on us.
Holy Mary,
Pray for us.
Holy Mother of God,
Pray for us.
Holy Virgin of Virgins,
Pray for us.
Mother of Christ,
Pray for us.
Mother of Divine Grace,
Pray for us.
Mother most chaste,
Pray for us.
Mother inviolate,
Pray for us.
Mother undefiled,
Pray for us.
Mother most amiable,
Pray for us.

Mother most admirable,
Pray for us.
Mother of good counsel,
Pray for us.
Mother of our Creator,
Pray for us.
Mother of our Savior,
Pray for us.
Virgin most prudent,
Pray for us.
Virgin most venerable,
Pray for us.
Virgin most renowned,
Pray for us.
Virgin most powerful,
Pray for us.
Virgin most merciful,
Pray for us.
Virgin most faithful,
Pray for us.
Mirror of justice,
Pray for us.
Seat of wisdom,
Pray for us.
Cause of our joy,
Pray for us.
Vessel of honor,
Pray for us.
Singular vessel of devotion,
Pray for us.
Mystical Rose,
Pray for us.

Tower of David,
Pray for us.
Tower of ivory,
Pray for us.
House of gold,
Pray for us.
Ark of the Covenant,
Pray for us.
Gate of Heaven,
Pray for us.
Morning star,
Pray for us.
Health of the sick,
Pray for us.
Refuge of sinners,
Pray for us.
Comforter of the afflicted,
Pray for us.
Help of Christians,
Pray for us.
Queen of angels,
Pray for us.
Queen of patriarchs,
Pray for us.
Queen of prophets,
Pray for us.
Queen of Apostles,
Pray for us.
Queen of martyrs,
Pray for us.
Queen of confessors,
Pray for us.

Queen of virgins,
Pray for us.
Queen of all saints,
Pray for us.
Queen conceived without original sin,
Pray for us.
Queen assumed into Heaven,
Pray for us.
Queen of the Most Holy Rosary,
Pray for us.
Queen of Peace,
Pray for us.
Lamb of God, who takes away the sins of the world,
Spare us, O Lord.
Lamb of God, who takes away the sins of the world
Graciously hear us O Lord.
Lamb of God, who takes away the sins of the world
Have mercy on us.
Pray for us, O holy Mother of God.
That we may be made worthy of the Promises of Christ.
Let us pray.
Grant, O Lord God, we beseech Thee, that we Thy servants may rejoice in continual health of mind and body; and, through the glorious intercession of Blessed Mary ever Virgin, may be freed from present sorrow, and enjoy eternal gladness. Through Christ our Lord. Amen.

Here is an online link for the [Litany of the Blessed Mother](www.ourcatholicprayers.com/litany-of-the-blessed-virgin-mary.html) (www.ourcatholicprayers.com/litany-of-the-blessed-virgin-mary.html).

There are two sisters who joined me and we became long time bible study friends. One sister shared with me that she also had a reawakening of her Blessed Mother devotion through the Medjugorje apparition. Ever since that experience in the 80's she has faithfully prayed her Rosary. At times a small group of family and friends would gather at home to pray the Rosary. She feels praying the Rosary has increased her love for Our Lord in the Eucharist by attending daily Mass and oftentimes Eucharist Adoration. Also stronger devotion to the Blessed Mother and her statue.

The other sister feels she's always had a long time love for Our Lady and has memories when she was a little girl in her family, hearing the Litany of Loreto being prayed. Not even knowing what "House of Gold" meant. It was something that became ingrained in her. Gradually in her adult years and having her own family she became more devoted to praying the Rosary to seek support from Our Lady maintaining the family life. Her love for daily Mass is attributed to all those years praying the Rosary.

Now the two sisters as of recent joined again to support and participate in the morning Rosary group oftentimes to pray six days a week before daily Mass!

My cousin is currently taking care of her partner who is very ill at here home and under heavy medications. She pretty much handles everything, taking care of him, the household and her apartment building as landlord. She looks forward to her evenings and that can be late through the night. That's when she prays her Rosary to give her comfort and peace that could be 3 am. She keeps several little prayer books about the Rosary and other prayers on her nightstand for ease of comfort. She can remember praying her rosary all her life, even to the time when she was a little girl and her mom's next door neighbor would at times call out to my cousin who was playing and ask her if she'd like to come over and pray the Rosary. She would answer - yes!

CHAPTER 7

Various ways to pray the Holy Rosary

All glorious is the King's daughter as she enters;
her raiment is threaded with spun gold
(Psalm 44:14)

He created me in eternity, before time began
and I will exist for all eternity to come
(Sirach 24:9)

In this section, we'll cover other ways you can pray the Rosary, without the Rosary beads if you like, since it may not be possible to use them, for example, driving a car. Before Covid, I used to travel for my job and drive to different company locations. I like to start my day with a rosary, using my cellphone connected to the car stereo, listening to and following a Rosary recording.

Which way will you choose to pray the Rosary? Maybe you already pray using your favorite Rosary beads, perhaps one you've had for years, or it's a new one you got as a gift, or maybe you treated yourself. Do you pray it alone, or in a group such as in church? Hopefully by the time you read this, the church pandemic restrictions have been lifted. It is very commendable and beautiful if you are praying alone, but if you pray it in a group there are tremendous Graces given. In St. Louis de Montfort's book, *The Secret of the Rosary*, in the forty-sixth Rose regarding Group Recitation, he says, "Of all the ways of saying the Holy Rosary, the most glorious to God, most salutary to our souls, and the most terrible to the Devil is that of saying or chanting the Rosary publicly in two choirs. God is very pleased to have people gathered together in prayer. That is why the first Christians met together so often, in spite of the persecutions of the emperors who forbade them to assemble. They preferred to risk death rather than to miss gatherings where Our Lord was present."

The law of public prayer according to St. Louis is: "One who says their Rosary alone gains the merit of that one Rosary. But if he says it together with thirty others, he gains the merit of thirty Rosaries."[6]

There are stories of the faithful on their deathbed who tell their family they prayed a million Rosaries over the course of their lifetime. Do you think that person skipped Purgatory and went directly to heaven?

Here's an example from de Montfort's book, a testament to the power of the Rosary when you die. St. Dominic had been giving advice about the Rosary graces to a pious woman, who was devout and fervent, even putting on sackcloth for penance. But she would not take the advice. He writes, "Then when she was at prayer she fell into ecstasy, appearing before the Supreme Judge. St. Michael put all her penances and other prayers on one side of the scales and all her sins and imperfections on the other. The tray of her good works was greatly outweighed by that of her sins and imperfections. Filled with alarm, she cried for mercy, imploring the help of the Blessed Virgin, her gracious Advocate, who took the one and only Rosary the woman had said for her penance and dropped it on the tray of her good works. This one Rosary was so heavy that it weighed more than all her sins as well as her good works. After Our Lady reproved her, when she came to herself, she threw herself at St. Dominic's feet, promising to say the Rosary every day. By this means she rose to Christian perfection and finally to the glory of everlasting life."[7]

Think of the wonderful Graces you could attain if you joined or started a Rosary group and held it before Mass started, for example a daily Mass. Ask the pastor! Tremendous graces can be given by Our Lady and Our Lord by praying the Rosary, attending Holy Mass, and receiving the Eucharist. It is a plenary indulgence. Speaking of indulgences, if you think its pittance, like the pittance you give to the poor, think of indulgences as pittance and give it to the poor souls in Purgatory. They'll literally be eternally grateful and will remember you when you die. Just think if you could couple those powerhouses with monthly Confession. You would be hitting the four most important principles of practicing the faith extraordinaire: 1) Holy Mass, 2) Holy Eucharist, 3) Confession, 4) Holy Rosary. Just praying the Rosary on its own is a sign of predestination. Read on to learn how that can be.

Nowadays, most everyone has a smartphone. Do you have the YouTube app? If you don't, think about getting it from the app store. Then you can find and watch videos of the Rosary. Just type in the YouTube search box "Pray the Rosary." and you'll get a listing of Rosaries said by individuals or groups in English, Spanish, Polish, or just about any language you want. You can also use your computer to Google, "Rosary videos" and you will get a long list of them. Watch them while sitting at home, or play them with headphones while walking or biking, or listen through your car stereo while driving. If your drive is a 15 to 20 minute round trip or longer, you can do a whole Rosary. Or you can relax in your backyard, listen, and pray with your beads.

Another option is to save your favorite Rosaries on your smart phone. At the bottom of the video you'll find either a "save" icon or a "share" icon, and from there you can save it to create your own playlist, or share it with others.

Maybe you have discussed the Promises and Graces of the Rosary from the Blessed Mother with someone you are evangelizing, and now you can share it with them. Our Lady has a Promise for those who propagate the Rosary!

I have saved videos of all the Mysteries said traditionally, but also Scriptural Rosaries where a Scripture verse is said before praying the next Hail Mary. The Traditional Rosaries are about 15 minutes long, and the Scriptural Rosaries last about 22 minutes. Right now at our parish, because of the pandemic, we even have the Blessed Sacrament visible through a window. You can drive up, have Eucharistic Adoration, and pray the Rosary right in the car.

Suppose you like to exercise, or you run or walk because you need the physical benefit. I know I do. I realized I needed to walk for the exercise, so I decided to walk to church for daily Mass. It's a two-mile walk round trip. I pocketed my smartphone with my Rosary video, got out my headphones, and began praying the Rosary while walking to Mass. Once I was at church, I joined a group to pray the Rosary again before Holy Mass.

You've probably figured out that I'm at a point in life when my wife and I are empty nesters. We plan to continue to prepare, save, and preserve for the future as long as we live—though God only knows what will happen to this world. Now more than ever, we feel the need to prepare and preserve, building treasure for the afterlife. God willing, and with the help of the Blessed Mother whose side we never want to leave, we aim for Heaven. We hold onto the Promise of the Blessed Mother for deliverance from Purgatory by—you guessed it—praying the Rosary daily. I urge you to create or join a Rosary group, preferably at church before Holy Mass.

Of course if you're young and married, working or taking care of children, it can be hard to get to weekday Mass. If you can, try to form a family Rosary. It reminds me of the time when our kids were little and we had family Rosary every week with other families. We had social time afterwards, kind of like a Sunday game day used to be before the pandemic.

Various ways to pray the Holy Rosary

※

Back in the 1990s working downtown, I met up with a friend who also loved the Rosary, and after lunch while we took a walk, we prayed the Rosary under our breaths for sinners everywhere. We need more prayer warriors walking the neighborhoods today, blessing them with Hail Marys. We need thousands of prayer warriors praying the Rosary in the city streets to fight the evil that is currently overcoming our cities.

As an example, Father Donald H. Calloway of the Marians of the Immaculate Conception, has written several beautiful books on the Rosary. In his latest book, *The Wonders of the Rosary*, he writes, "In Brazil in 1964, when the country was governed by a communist-leaning President Joao Goulart, large groups of people turned to the Rosary and rose up in rebellion against their oppressive leaders. Rosary groups formed and were able to break up communist rallies by marching in the streets, loudly praying the Rosary. Afterward, the president ridiculed the Rosary, saying his communist ideas would save Brazil, not the rosaries of simple women. These words greatly upset the Brazilian people. At one of the communist rallies, more than 20,000 women marched into the streets with rosaries in their hands to engage in a spiritual battle. They marched right into the midst of the communist rally and prayed the Rosary so loudly that it shut the rally down. Only six days after that, more than 600,000 people marched through the streets. Since they changed the name of the rally to March of the Family with God toward Freedom, many non Catholics attended the march and prayed the rosary with the Catholics." The end of the story is even better. The president fled the country, and in gratitude to Our Lady, a million people marched in a "March of Thanksgiving to God."[8] (9)

Please note who started the Rosary march—it was 20,000 women. Where were the Knights?

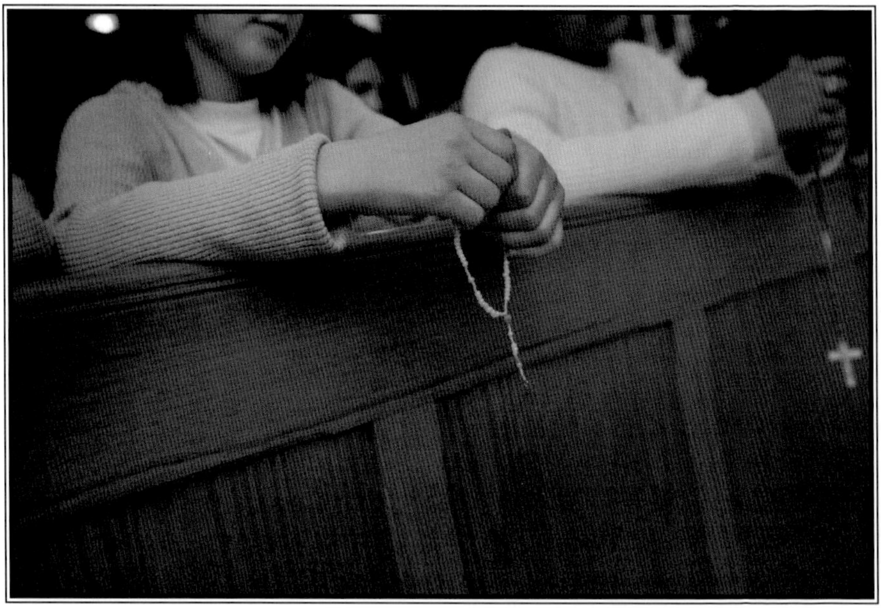

CHAPTER 8

Promises from Heaven

❧

*Listen, I have something important to tell
you, when I speak, my words are right*
(Proverbs 8:6)

*My words are all straight to him who understands
and right to those who find knowledge*
(Proverbs 8:9)

Below are the Fifteen Promises of Mary granted to those who pray the Rosary. These were imparted by Our Lady to Saint Dominic and Blessed Alan.

Please read these Promises very slowly to get a thorough understanding of their blessings. I recommend returning to them after some time has passed to remind yourself. You may discover a new light on a promise you hadn't considered before. That's how beautiful the Promises can be.

The Fifteen Promises of Mary

1. Whoever shall faithfully serve me by the recitation of the Rosary shall receive signal graces.

2. I promise my special protection and the greatest graces to all those who shall recite the Rosary.
3. The Rosary shall be a powerful armor against Hell; it will destroy vice, decrease sin, and defeat heresies.
4. The Rosary will cause virtue and good works to flourish, it will obtain for souls the abundant Mercy of God, it will withdraw the hearts of men from the love of the world and its vanities and will lift them to the desire for eternal things. Oh, that souls would sanctify themselves by this means.
5. The soul which recommends itself to me by the recitation of the Rosary shall not perish
6. Whoever shall recite the Rosary devoutly, applying himself to the consideration of it's sacred mysteries shall never be conquered by misfortune. God will not chastise him in His justice, he shall not perish by an unprovided death, if he be just he shall remain in the Grace of God and become worthy of eternal life.
7. Whoever shall have a true devotion for the Rosary shall not die without the Sacraments of the Church.
8. Those who are faithful to recite the Rosary shall have during their life and at their death the Light of God and the plentitude of His Graces; at the moment of death they shall participate in the merits of the Saints in paradise.
9. I shall deliver from Purgatory those who have been devoted to the Rosary.
10. The faithful children of the Rosary shall merit a high degree of glory in Heaven.
11. You shall obtain all you ask of me by the recitation of the Rosary.
12. All those who propagate the Holy Rosary shall be aided by me in their necessities.

13. I have obtained from my Divine Son that all the advocates of the Rosary shall have for intercessors the entire Celestial Court during their life and at the hour of death.
14. All who recite the Rosary are my sons and daughters, and brothers and sisters of my only Son, Jesus Christ.
15. Devotion of my Rosary is a great sign of predestination.

You can find them listed online here:

Most Holy Rosary (www.themostholyrosary.com)

A website with extensive information on the Rosary is How To Pray The Rosary (www.how-to-pray-the-rosary-everyday.com). I especially like that you can translate the website into any language. Polish or Spanish anyone?

A great website shop for purchasing your rosaries, sacramentals, or prayer books is here: Twelve St. Bridget Prayers (www.catholicshoppeusa.com/products/st-bridget-twelve-year-prayers-on-the-passion-of-jesus). There is a favorite Rosary prayer tri-fold booklet I like to order for evangelizing. It's the 12-year St. Bridget prayer on the Passion of Our Lord Jesus Christ and the Seven Sorrows of our Blessed Mother Rosary.

You can also access it at the top right in the search box: type in "Twelve" and the first on the list should be the booklet. The Promises from Our Lady and Our Lord are for doing these prayers daily, and are tremendous blessings for you and your future generations. In addition, you might like to find a YouTube video to help you pray for the Seven Sorrows of Our Mother as it presents the Sorrows she endured during Our Lord's time.

My favorite in English is a rose-colored video title " The Seven Sorrows Rosary" It has beautiful background music to listen to as you pray the Rosary with it. The video images are beautiful on the Mysteries as you meditate on them.

If you are in a Rosary group at church or plan to join or create one, consider substituting the Seven Sorrows Rosary for one of the days Tuesday or Friday as those are the days the Sorrowful Mysteries Rosary are prayed. Doing the Seven Sorrows Rosary will help you meditate on the Mysteries as seen through Our Blessed Mother's eyes. The Blessed Mother's promises to those who pray the Seven Sorrows Rosary, according to St. Bridget, are:

The Seven Sorrows of our Blessed Mother

1. I will grant peace to their families.
2. They will be enlightened about the divine Mysteries.
3. I will console them in their pains and I will accompany them in their work.
4. I will give them as much as they ask for as long as it does not oppose the adorable will of my divine Son or the sanctification of their souls.
5. I will defend them in their spiritual battles with the infernal enemy and I will protect them at every instant of their lives.
6. I will visibly help them at the moment of their death - they will see the face of their Mother.
7. I have obtained this Grace from My divine Son, that those who propagate this devotion to my tears and sorrows will be taken directly from this earthly life to eternal happiness, since all their sins will be forgiven and My Son will be their eternal consolation and joy.

You can find the Seven Sorrows prayers at Church Pop (www.church-pop.com).Following are the Promises given to St. Bridget by Our Divine Lord to whoever meditates on the seven times that Christ shed His Precious Blood on our account. When the set of prayers are said daily for 12 years (I'm doing lifetime) these five Graces are promised:

The Promises of Our Divine Lord given to St. Bridget

1. The soul who prays them suffers no Purgatory.
2. The souls who pray them will be accepted among the Martyrs as though they had spilled their blood for their faith.
3. The souls who pray them can choose three others whom Jesus will then keep in a state of Grace sufficient to become holy.
4. No one in the four successive generations of the soul who prays them will be lost.
5. The soul who prays them will be made conscious of his death one month in advance. If the suppliant should die before the allotted span, God the Father will accept them as having been prayed in their entirety, as the genuine intention was there. If a day or a few days are missed for a valid reason, they can be made up later.

This devotion was pronounced good and profitable as treasures in Heaven and recommended by both the Sacred Congregation for the Propagation of the Faith—The Holy Office—and by Pope Clement XII. Pope Innocent X declared that the Promises are from God.

You can find these prayers and promises online here: Saint Bridget's Prayers Devotion for twelve years - seven prayers (www.theworkofgod.org/Devotns/bridget_12years.htm). Need we say more on these Promises that are like gold for our souls?

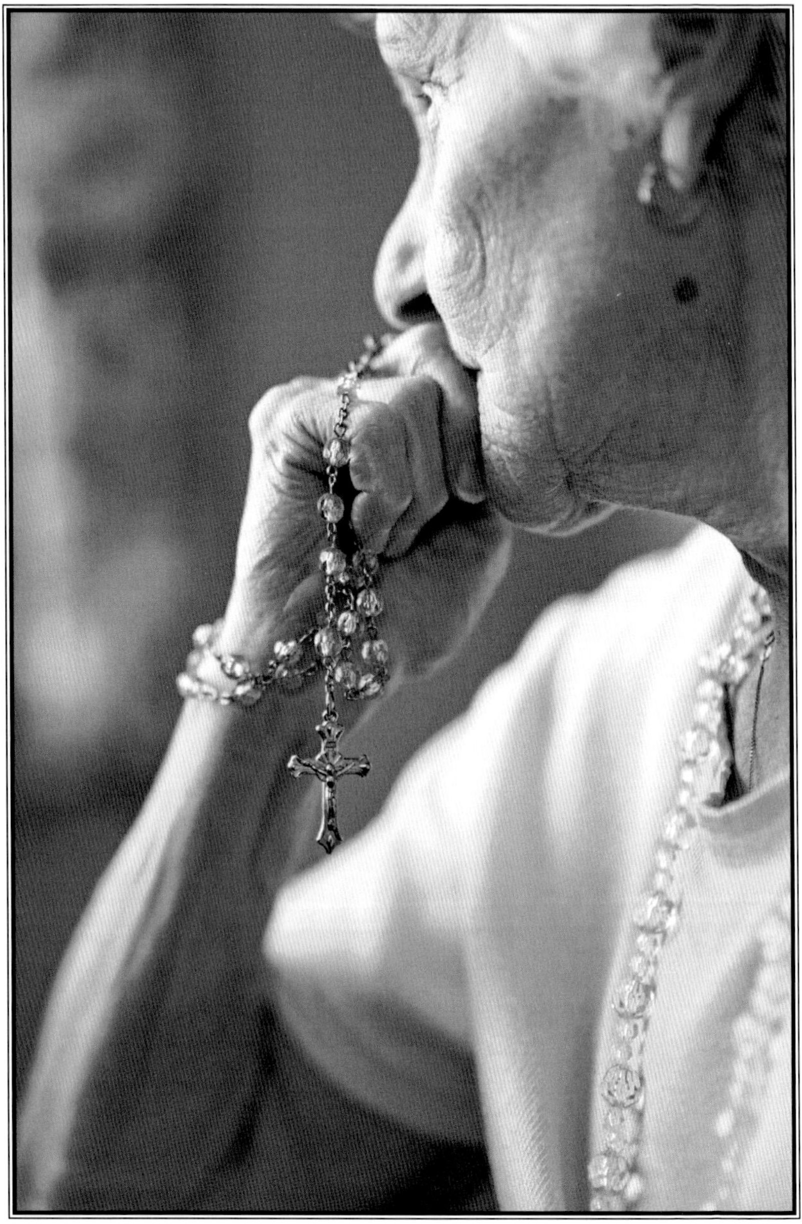

CHAPTER 9
Mystical Rose

On the heights overlooking the road, at the crossways, she takes her stand
(Proverbs 8:2)

Happy are those who keep my ways, watching daily at my gates
(Proverbs 8:3)

THE MYSTICAL CITY OF GOD

We have immersed ourselves in how beautiful the Rosary is in its excellence and its simplicity. But it is important to understand why our Blessed Mother holds such an important role in the salvation of souls. I'd like to briefly refer to a book on Our Lady written by the Venerable Mary of Ágreda called *The Mystical City of God*, in Spanish *Ciudad de Dios*. You can find it here: <u>Mystical City of God - Virgin Mary</u> (www.theworkofgod.org/Mystical-City-of-God.htm).

The new edition in 1949 was given the Imprimatur—permission to be published—by Archbishop Edwin V. Byrne. This was a reprint from the original authorized 1902 Spanish edition without change, already bearing the Imprimatur of Bishop H.J. Alerding. The work itself went under intense scrutiny forty years after the first appearance of the *Ciudad de Dios*. The great universities of Europe were called upon to give their opinion about this great work, as well as the learned men and teachers of each religious Order that maintained institutions of learning in Europe. Fifteen Orders complied, including: The Augustinians, Benedictines, Carmelites, Dominicans, Jesuits, Cistercians. All unanimously endorsed the favorable decision previously published by the University of Salamanca. To summarize the official approbation from the University of Louvain, "We have come to the conclusion that it will be most useful for enlivening and augmenting the piety of the faithful, the veneration of the Holy Virgin, and the respect for the Sacred Mysteries."[9] Lastly, Decrees were given by Pope Innocent XI in 1686, followed by decrees by Popes Alexander VIII, Clement IX, Benedict XIII, Benedict XIV, and Clement XIV. All to officially establish the authenticity of *Ciudad de Dios*.[10]

Since this is considered private revelation which you can believe or not, as mentioned earlier regarding apparitions, I referenced the above to illustrate that we may not want to take this writing lightly, as to whether it's true or not. Having said that, I'd like to highlight just a few excerpts from the very lengthy four-volume work.

Starting with *Book Three*, it highlights that the Rosary "Contains the most exquisite preparations of the Almighty for the Incarnation of the Word in Mary Most Holy." In this text it is proper that Mary, as the Mother of the Divine Word uniting man and God, should bear a relation to both.[11] A second reason is because her most Holy Son was Himself to obey this Heavenly Queen, His Mother. Since He was the creator of the elements and of all things, it follows naturally that they should also obey her. Was it not the Person of Christ Himself, insofar as His human nature was concerned, to be governed by His Mother according to the constitution and the laws of nature?[12]

Also in *Book Three* the title reads "(Satan) with all his seven legions, persists in tempting Most Holy Mary; she conquers the dragon and crushes his head." In section #365, "The Almighty gave into the hands of our Victorious Chieftainess the sword for cutting off the head of the infernal dragon; a power never to be diminished in her, and with which she defends and assists the Militant Church according to the labors and necessities of coming centuries."

Let's pause here before we continue. We've known Our Lady as being the Mother of God, Jesus Christ her Son, and now in the truest sense of the Word, as implicitly stated and recognized, A part of Him is in her and a part of her is in Him. Another revelation is made in section #368 in relation to Genesis 3:15, "She shall crush thy head, and thou shalt lie in wait for her heel." The Almighty Father gave the sword to Our Lady.

The Catholic faithful are members of the Church Militant, Our Lord is the Head. However, we now see it is Our Lady who has been given the sword, the power, and the mission to crush the head of Satan. Fr. Donald Calloway has written close to 15 books on Our Blessed Mother and the Rosary, and on the website <u>Catholic Exchange</u> (www.catholic-exchange.com/rosary-spiritual-sword-mary) he writes, "The blade of this sword was forged in the living Word of God, shaped by the hammer of Divine Inspiration, and entrusted to the Queen Of Heaven and her chosen servants."[13]

We know the story—one of her chosen servants was St. Dominic, but it can also be you. It is befitting that Our Lady is called Virgin Most Powerful. Our Lord Jesus Christ is our Savior who calls us to follow him. It is our cross to bear. In the end though, when we die and enter into our judgement, it is Our Lord who is now our Judge. It is our Queen of Heaven who promises that when we pray the Rosary, she will be at our side. We are in a constant spiritual battle, so why would we not want to be right now on her side, and she on ours?

In Book Eight, chap 22, verse #778 reads "Thou shall be the Special Patroness of the Catholic countries, and whenever they, or the faithful, or any of the children of Adam, call upon thee from their heart, serve, or oblige thee, thou shalt relieve and help them in their labors and necessities. Thou shalt be the Friend, the Defender, and the Chieftainess of all the just and of our friends; all of them thou shalt comfort, console, and fill with blessings according to their devotion to thee. In view of all this We make thee the Depositary of Our Riches, the Treasurer of our goods; we place into thy hands the Help and Blessings of Our Grace for distribution; nothing do We wish to be given to the world which does not pass through thy hands; and nothing do We deny, which thou wishes to concede men. Grace shall be diffused in thy lips for obtaining all that thou wishest and ordainest in heaven and on earth, and everywhere shall angels and men obey thee; because whatever is Ours shall be theirs, just as thou hast always been Ours, and thou shalt reign with Us forever."[14]

There you have it, this verse #778 coincides with what the Venerable Fulton Sheen wrote: "Jesus is the Mediator between God and humanity; Our Lord is the Mediator between God and man; Mary is the Mediatrix between Jesus and us."[15] Doesn't your heart yearn to be devoted, to consecrate yourself to Our Blessed Mother?

St. Alphonsus Liguori's book, *The Glories of Mary* is in three parts. The first part consists of chapters dedicated to the prayer "Hail Holy Queen." Each chapter is a beautiful description of each verse of the prayer. The second part contains decrees, each describing Mary's life and role as Mediatrix, from the Presentation of Mary at the Temple in the beginning, to her Queenship in Heaven. The third part tells about the Sorrows of Our Blessed Mother. It is another exceptional book on Our Lady.

I'd like to highlight section one, page 82. The title is "Mary is our Life," because she obtains pardon for our sins. In order to understand the reason why the Holy Church calls Mary our life, we must consider that as the soul gives life to the body, so Divine Grace gives life to the soul; for a soul without Grace, though nominally alive, in truth is dead. As Mary by her intercession obtains for sinners, the gift of Grace, she restores them to life. The Holy Church applies to her the following words in Proverbs. "They that in the morning watch for me, shall find me. They shall find me," or, according to the Septuagint, "They shall find Grace." Hence, to have recourse to Mary is to find the Grace of God, for as immediately follows, "He who finds me shall find life and shall receive from God eternal salvation." To summarize, it's Jesus through Mary.

A copy of St. Alphonsus's book can be found here:

The Glories of Mary
(www.themostholyrosary.com/the-glories-of-mary.pdf)

Perhaps now you understand what Our Lady is offering you. Praying the Rosary has countless graces for you. But, also consider all the good you can do for your loved ones as you pray for them. Consider the Rosary helping the poor souls and sinners everywhere, combating evil. The list is endless! That's how powerful and yet how simple the Rosary is for us.

I quote the following passage by Carlos Caso-Rosendi in his book *Guadalupe, A River of Light* to illustrate the point of the Rosary and Our Lady's calling. "When the river issuing from the mouth of the dragon threatens to drown us all, when all that is firm and steady collapses all around us and we are standing alone before the Cross, we will take strength in Our Lady just like the Christian fighters of old, and many others who had to face their own personal apocalypse. The river of impurity and death issuing from the Devil is countered by this other river of light, the river of countless graces flowing from the blessed hands of

Our Lady. She will generously dispense those graces and help us heal our world if we would only ask her!"

If you would like to fully engage in the spiritual battle, you could join the Auxilium Christianorum, which was founded to wage war against the demonic forces. The website is here (www.auxiliumchristianorum.org). Membership is free, however please read the requirements of members. One is to consult with a spiritual director or confessor. Read the prayers, and if you feel confident in the Lord and Our Blessed Mother, then carry on soldier! There is also an app available for your phone. This is a prayer from the Auxilium to again illustrate Our Lady's mission:

AUGUST QUEEN OF THE HEAVENS

August Queen of the Heavens, heavenly Sovereign of the Angels, thou who from the beginning has received from God the power and mission to crush the head of Satan, we humbly beseech thee to send thy holy legions, so that under thy command and through thy power they may pursue the demons and combat them everywhere, suppress their boldness, and drive them back into the abyss. O good and tender Mother, thou wilt always be our love and hope! O Divine Mother, send thy Holy Angels to defend us and to drive far away from us the cruel enemy. Holy Angels and Archangels, defend us, guard us. Amen.

Here is a link to their prayers:

Auxilium Christianorum
(www.auxiliumchristianorum.org/wp-content/
uploads/2018/04/dailyprayers.pdf).

A mom who attends daily Mass with her four year old son when she can, recently informed me that her family uses Zoom video with her family in Mexico. They pray the Rosary via Zoom and like to pray the Seven Sorrows Rosary booklet in Spanish. The family in Mexico loved it and sent back another Spanish version that's deeper in prayers. Talk about using technology!

Some of you have now made the wonderful decision to answer Our Lady's call. There are others who may have stopped praying the Rosary but hopefully will now start up again. And there are surely others who have always prayed the Rosary, but maybe you have at least learned something new. It's all good and done for Our Lady and Our Lord.

I hope you now feel a greater love for Our Lady and wish to do more, or would even like to learn how to give yourself totally, as St. John Paul II lovingly said, "*Totus Tuus!*" which means "Totally Yours!" The way to become totally hers is through a preparation for Consecration to Mary. I suggest obtaining the St. Louis de Montfort book which outlines the method for preparation, which is called "Total Consecration to Jesus through Mary." You can order an eBook version or a paperback at an online store or through your favorite Christian bookstore.

Another good book for Consecration is *Mary's Mantle Consecration* by Christine Watkins, which is available in English or Spanish. Here are the links: Mary's Mantle Consecration (www.amazon.com/dp/1947701061/) and El Manto de María Una Consagración (www.amazon.com/dp/1947701169/). It would be a very good practice to renew your Consecration to Our Lady once a year.

<hr />

On the other end of the spectrum, if you would like to reach out to your community about the fruits of the Rosary and the message of Our Mother at Fatima, you could join the organization America Needs Fatima, become a captain, and organize a Rosary rally in your neighborhood. It's voluntary, and it's much needed to combat evil.

At this website you can find all the information for both English and Spanish rallies:

America Needs Fatima
(www.americaneedsfatima.org/Rally-News/rosary-rally-central-2.html).

There are dozens of Catholic Rosary movements you can be a part of. I've already mentioned the America Needs Fatima program, and then there's the Rosary Confraternity, of which I'm a member. Or you can join Marian Helpers thru the Marian Fathers, where you will find Father Donald Calloway and Father Chris Alar. Father Alar also has some excellent video classes on the Catholic Faith, especially about the Divine Mercy message. Those organizations can be found here: Rosary Center (www.rosarycenter.org), and here: The Divine Mercy (www.thedivinemercy.org)

Epilogue

In this book I give witness of my love for the Blessed Mother. I wanted to write the book because you might be seeing how the forces of darkness have permeated most forms of communication and information today, including television networks, social media, mass media, books, music, art, as well as the push to change our history, including our Catholic faith and traditions. Social and political movements calling for change are moving fast. We are surely entering a spiritual battle, although no one is calling to march in the streets…yet.

Thankfully, Our Lady is the Mediatrix between souls and the Holy Trinity. The Holy Rosary is the sword for spiritual combat. We on earth are prayer warriors, and evangelizers bringing more faithful to the Blessings and Promises of the Holy Rosary. Only Holy Mass and the Sacraments hold more importance for our faith. We are all called to Proclaim the Gospel.

It is easy to pray the Rosary, whichever way you choose to do so. It only takes 15 to 20 minutes of your day. Praying the Rosary in a group setting is even more bountiful for your salvation.

Our Blessed Mother will not fail us, individually or collectively. "In the End My Immaculate Heart will Triumph." Let us shout to the world what we say to the Blessed Queen: "*Totus Tuus ego sum!*" I am all yours!

References

1. St. Louis de Montfort, *The Secret of the Rosary, Second Rose*, trans. Mary Barbour TOP Bay Shore, NY: Montfort Publications, 1988, p 12

2. St. Louis de Montfort, *The Secret of the Rosary, Sixth Rose*, trans. Mary Barbour TOP Bay Shore, NY: Montfort Publications, 1988, pp 19-20

3. St. Louis de Montfort, *The Secret of the Rosary, Seventh Rose*, trans. Mary Barbour TOP Bay Shore, NY: Montfort Publications, 1988, p 19

4. Ven. Fulton J. Sheen, *The World's First Love: Mary Mother of God*, San Francisco, CA, Ignatius Press, 1996, pp 207-208

5. Philip Kosoloski, *Nine Saints who loved praying the Rosary*, 08-10-18, www.Aleteia.org

6. St. Louis de Montfort, *The Secret of the Rosary, forty-sixth Rose*, trans. Mary Barbour TOP Bay Shore, NY, Montfort Publications, 1988, pp 76-77

7. St. Louis de Montfort, *The Secret of the Rosary, forty-sixth Rose*, trans. Mary Barbour TOP Bay Shore, NY: Montfort Publications, 1988, pp 48-49

8. Fr. Donald H. Calloway, *Wonders of the Rosary*, Marian Fathers of the Immaculate Conception of B.V.M., Marian Helpers Center, 2019, pp 78-81

9. Venerable Mary of Ágreda, *Mystical City of God*, Tan Books, 1978, Location 138 of 10009

10. Venerable Mary of Ágreda, *Mystical City of God*, Tan Books, 1978, Location 181 of 10009

11. Venerable Mary of Ágreda, *Mystical City of God*, Tan Books, 1978, eBook, Book 3, Chapter 2 #16

12. Venerable Mary of Ágreda, *Mystical City of God*, Tan Books, 1978, eBook, Book 3, Chapter 2 #20

13. Father Donald H. Calloway, www.CatholicExchange.com/Rosary-Spiritual-Sword-Mary

14. Venerable Mary of Ágreda, *Mystical City of God*, Tan Books, 1978, eBook, Book 8, Chapter 22 #778

15. Venerable Fulton J. Sheen, *The World's First Love: Mary Mother of God*, San Francisco, CA, Ignatius Press, 1996, p 49